LUCKY WITH MONEY

A Real Mom's Guide to Taking Care of Your Money

ZAHRA KHAKOO

WHEN IT COMES TO
SUCCESS...

MONEY IS 20%

KNOWLEDGE &
BEHAVIOR 80%

Zahra

Book Layout © Million-Dollar-Author 2021

Lucky With Money -- 1st edition.

ISBN: 978-0-6450942-9-9

TESTIMONIALS FOR ZAHRA AND THE BOOK LUCKY WITH MONEY

Thank you once again for your guidance and mentorship over the last few months. I have so appreciated your candor and advice as well as your realistic assessment of my finances and willingness to support me as I undertook this aggressive reorganization. I am so pleased with the results

Belinda – Financial mastery course participant

I just received my latest credit report notifying that a change happened in my credit score. It has gone up from 600 – 725. I am thrilled and feel as though I am finally adulting now... and just shy of 45 years old, I suppose that although I am late to the party, I am doing good all things considered. Thank you for the coaching you have provided to get me here.

Lauren – Coaching Client

Introduction

As a Financial professional, time and time again, I would see women who would auto default to let their husbands handle financial aspects of their lives. This is not only detrimental to them in the long term but also leaves them feeling helpless when something bad happens like divorce or death. My book will help empower every woman with skills they need so that no matter what life throws at you financially-you can take charge!

This book will be a great resource for women to turn to. We all know that finances can be difficult, but having resources available makes overcoming daunting obstacles easier and less stressful. I find that it is always handy to have more than one opinion when investing my money. Sometimes friends and family aren't in the best place financially, which leaves you at a loss of who to trust with your hard earned dollars. It is important for every woman to know how take care of themselves financially so that they can be confident in managing it on their own even if they don't have someone else there with them anymore; this why I wrote my book "Lucky With Money"

Dedication

To my daughter Ziyanna
Come rain or shine, I will always be by your side.

To all the women who will read this
You are deserving of abundance in all areas of your life.

I would also like to Thank Brett Odgers and Billy McLean for their support and guidance throughout my whole book writing experience. This book would not have been possible without their support.

About the Author

Meet Zahra! She is a Solo Mom Coach, active mother, and a passionate advocate for widowed women after lost her own husband in 2015. All these roles have one thing in common, Zahra is a coach, cheerleader and motivator. She builds people up and puts her heart into helping others bounce back from hard times.

Having learned the hard ways of how to take care of herself and her finances. Zahra holds a perspective that is so valuable and relatable. She broke through the "widow fog" to develop a financial system that helped her and now helps others. Her unique story allows her to truly empathize with her clients who are experiencing hardships.

CONTENTS

Chapter One

TAKING MY BREATH AWAY

It happens exactly as you imagine it would.

Your vision narrows, all sound is muted, and the world suddenly become very, very narrow. I really couldn't hear anything but my heartbeat, and it was ringing very loudly in my ears.

When I received the news that my husband had 6 months to live, everything changed. Nothing would ever be the same again. My mind raced forward and back as I came to grips with the consequences of what I had just heard. I began to instantly regret all the things we didn't do, the things we put off until later, and at the same time I begun to imagine all the things that he wouldn't have been a part of. Our daughter growing up, holidays and all the plans we made…. And then the tears started flowing. And wouldn't stop.

We found out my husband's cancer, which was in remission, was back and he had six months to live. There were many options and things we could have done, like flying to a specialized hospital in the United States (US) for treatment. That might have given us a little extra time, but not enough. And at a cost that was too high. He would be very sick from the treatment in our final months together. So, we made a decision to just enjoy his last few months we had together as a family. And that's a decision that I'm grateful for every day.

We both stopped working and just spent time together. We had time to fulfil one last dream of a family vacation together. My daughter was four and a half and had never been to Disneyland. We were waiting for her to get to around eight years old because we felt that memory would be stronger, but my husband said he wanted to be the one to take her to Disneyland.

It was the biggest and hardest decision we made, because we could have stayed and used our funds and time to do treatment. We decided to spend a bit of those funds going to Disneyland, and the rest for my daughter's education and our future.

On the Disney trip, we spared no expense. We did the character breakfast, we stayed at a nice hotel, and did everything we could. This would be one of the last times we would all be together, and we wanted it to be a dream holiday. My daughter is now 11 years old, and this holiday is her fondest memory. With two of the most important abiding memories forever linked. Disney and her Dad.

For my husband and I, it was a sad holiday, but also a good one. Even though he was sick and couldn't participate in a lot of things, he was there for a lot of it, and we had a lot of fun. Anytime my daughter and I talk about him, Disney comes up.

The following years have not been easy for either me or my daughter. Losing my husband, and her dad, shook our world. One of the most important things that we learnt was the importance of memories and investing in the right things.

When talking about money and investment, most people tell you to invest in this or that class of asset. But for human beings, the most valuable investment you will make is creating memories for you, and the people most important to you. Whether that is going to Disney, taking your dream holiday, or bringing them all to you, investment in memories pays off at a magnitude like no other investment class ever.

We could easily have put a deposit on a property, or purchased something we'd always wanted, but those things fade with time. Memories not only live forever, but actually become more valuable with time. Their value increases the longer you have them. The return on that investment is forever, and it was one of the wisest investments we ever made.

We were always savers. We lived in the house with his parents, so we didn't have to rent or have a mortgage or anything like that. The two of us worked, our funds came straight to us, and we invested it for our future. We worked for a secure future, until that future was taken away from us. So it was an easy decision to take that holiday to Disney.

The funds were available, so we didn't worry about going into debt. And when he decided he wanted to take us to Disneyland, within a couple of hours we had booked everything because we had no time to waste. Sometimes you can

The most valuable investment I ever made was in creating memories. That pays dividends for the rest of my daughter's life.

procrastinate on things like that, but we didn't have time.

Lucky with Money

Many people said we were so lucky with money, we were lucky my husband had insurance, and we were lucky to be able to rush off to Disneyland. But luck had nothing to do with it.

My husband was financially savvy and always thought about the future. He often said, maybe we should buy that this month, or maybe we should cut back on going out to eat this week. He was thoughtful about where each dollar went. That set us up for the future because we didn't know he would get sick. We thought we were saving for our retirement. But when he did get sick, because of these habits, we were already set up for a good future.

Most people go into a lot of debt trying to keep up with the Joneses, or to buy things for their children like cars and so on. They don't plan properly because they think they have plenty of time and things will always stay the same. Having investments and a saving mentality versus a spending mentality really helps with these kinds of unexpected things.

It's not just a death in the family that causes unexpected changes. 2020 saw the entire world plunged into a state of chaos. In my work in the financial sector, we see the result of this spending mentality every day. Businesses close because of debt; bankruptcies are soaring due to people never planning for the unexpected.

The culture right now is to use debt to get what you want instantly, which creates chains around people's ability to choose what they do. It ties them to jobs they don't like and locks them into situations they don't want because they used credit cards or other debt rather than investing in habits that make you *Lucky with Money*.

As I began to go solo after my husband died, I had to learn an entirely new way of doing things. Like so many couples, one of us was responsible for the money and the other could focus on other things. I had the luxury of leaving much of that to my husband. Unexpectedly alone, I now had to learn a new set of skills and look at life in a different way.

This book introduces habits and ways of thinking about being *Lucky with Money*. Especially for those that are going solo for the first time. If you think you are not lucky with money, we want to show you how to turn that around.

How I Became Lucky with Money

My parents moved to Canada from East Africa when my older sister was two and my mom was pregnant with my brother. They were refugees: my dad worked two jobs, and my Mom stayed home with the two kids. They had a hard time making ends meet.

When mom got pregnant with me it was stressful because they already had two kids. My parents did not want more kids because they had moved to a new country and were rebuilding. Times were tough. My Mom had an IUD which is supposed to be 99% effective. I was the 1%. When I was younger, they joked how I wasn't supposed to be. But when I came, their luck changed, so they said this child who wasn't supposed to be brought them luck.

They told me that my entire life that I was the lucky one. I wore brand new clothes when my siblings wore hand me downs. I was always told I was *Lucky with Money* so I never stressed about it because I always believed somehow it would happen because I am lucky.

My father started a business as a general contractor, fixing up properties and painting. My mother started a day home business, taking care of children in the home, so that she can be a stay-at-home mom, while still earning an income. Both of which took off when I was born. Mom ran that business for 30 years. Our house was the house where friends always came over, if kids were unhappy at home, they came to our house and got fed and taken care of. Even though there was scarcity, we always felt like there was abundance in our house. There was lots of food, people, and love to go around.

Being told I was lucky affected the way I thought about money and my whole view of the world. I had friends who were negative all the time, always thinking the worst of people, or what could happen. They were constantly stressed, which made matters worse, as they perpetuated those thoughts and things would go downhill for them.

If you believe there is only a finite amount of money, and once it is gone, there is no more, versus an abundance mindset where you feel it will come back, it is completely different. There is abundance in the world when it comes to money, but if you view it with a scarcity mindset, then you believe it will all end at some point.

Scarcity and abundance are economic theories put forward decades ago. They purported that in an economic system there were finite resources, and as a member of that system, your job was to get as big a piece of the pie as possible. Because there was only so much pie to go around, you had to fight for your bit of pie, otherwise you wouldn't get any. The scarcity theory has proven inaccurate and shown actually the more pie we eat, the more pie is created.

Abundance theory says the more we grow as people and as an economy, the more money there is to go around. It has been shown over and over to be a more accurate economic principle. Unfortunately, our education system suffers from a hangover of that scarcity mindset, and we believe it.

I had friends who were negative all the time, always thinking the worst of people. My parents told me I was lucky with money, and I was never stressed about it

It sounds plausible because professors say it is, but it isn't accurate. The research shows we live in the most abundant time in history with less poverty per capita, greater healthcare, and longer lives. There is abundance everywhere.

Unbeknownst to my parents, being told I was *Lucky with Money* growing up instilled an abundance mindset where I just had to look around, work out a way, and money would come. By taking a piece of the pie, you actually generate more.

For example, my Dad started a contracting business, earned more himself, but also employed people along the way. Not only did he get more money for himself and our family, he employed people who made money for their families.

In the theory of abundance, the more you do, the more you plan, the more you create, the more is created for everybody.

Tips for Staying in the Abundance Mindset

You need to believe you are lucky with money, that you will get more pieces of the pie, which will create more pieces of the pie, which could be infinite. But you can't just have that theory and think it will come, you have to have habits. You need to be frugal with money, save for the future, and really value each dollar. Each dollar should have a place to go so you are not spending it irrationally.

Actor and comedian Jim Carey famously said you can't visualize a Ferrari then go and make yourself a sandwich. You have to go and work for it. You can't have an abundance mindset then do nothing about it.

We have to begin to work on some skills, the mindset, and strategies to help you be luckier. This book will help you see the simple skills and habits anyone can implement to be luckier with money.

My husband had his devastating diagnosis and the future we thought we would have suddenly evaporated. All of these habits helped us live through that moment and into a much brighter future.

You might not have a husband who passes away, or another extreme circumstance like that, but you can build this confidence in your future to be able to bounce back from anything that happens.

When something like that happens, it is shocking to the heart, but money shouldn't be the thing you worry about as you take care of your loved ones.

That way you can focus on what is important, which is being there for your family. I could do that because we were set up. My husband had a backup plan. I was there 100% for my husband, we could walk away from our jobs and be with our daughter and enjoy our last few months together. This book is for everyone. All families should learn about the abundance mindset. If we believed we are lucky with money, we wouldn't have a lot of people crippled by debt, and everyone would live a nice, abundant life.

Three Outcomes of Learning to be Lucky with Money

You have the confidence to handle anything.
I didn't have to worry about money or working and could be there with my husband and daughter. I had the confidence to have the future I chose.

I was able to be confident when he passed. Because we had life insurance, I could purchase my own property, my daughter had an education fund set up, and my retirement fund was sorted. I didn't necessarily have to work as hard as some other widows do because of the loss of their spouse's income. It gave me confidence to live my new life the way I wanted.

Focus on what's important… And that shouldn't be money

You have control over your life.

You can choose what you want in life. Developing mastery over money can give you a sense of resilience.

When I got married, I worked as a banking professional. He thought I would do all the banking for our family. I thought in case something happened to me, he should learn this, so I gave the financials over to him to handle.

When our daughter arrived, I participated less and less. I did not have my finger on the pulse as I did in the beginning. When we got the six-month diagnosis, everything had to change. The light bulb went off, and I knew I had to figure everything out.

I didn't know our passwords, I didn't know where our money was, I didn't know what our investments were, I didn't have the whole picture. I spent time learning and relearning everything again.

Afterwards I struggled with the way my husband had money all over the place. It didn't work for me, so I consolidated everything into one place. Is it the best situation? I don't know, but it works. I only have two credit cards, vs that he had multiple cards, and accounts.

The Money Pyramid shows you the 3 areas to focus on to become luckier with money, Debt, Future Money and Fun Money. And what the outcomes are of getting it right

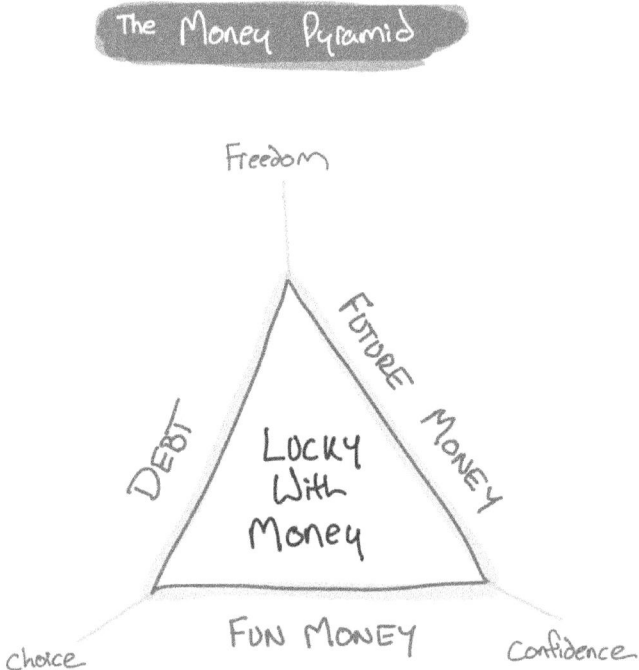

The Money Pyramid

Freedom

DEBT

FUTURE MONEY

LUCKY With Money

choice

FUN MONEY

Confidence

Doing all of this after the fact was difficult as I had to go everywhere with a death certificate and the will. Appointments were an hour or hour and a half versus if we had streamlined everything prior, it would have been easier.

When I took control, it was an amazing sense of accomplishment.

You have freedom.

Not necessarily the freedom of jetting off on a private jet or mega yacht, but to choose where you live, the work you want to do, the education you want for your children, and the freedom to take them to Disneyland.

A lot of women feel they don't have their own money, it's family money for the household, so they don't have the choice to make decisions by themselves. Many feel like they are working and working and working to make ends meet without hope for the future.

Once you have freedom of choice, it feels like the handcuffs are gone. They can choose what they want to do and the life they want for their family. If anything happens, they can choose what they want, and not be stuck because of money issues.

It doesn't have to be a disaster, it can be as simple as an amazing opportunity you always wanted, like going to the country, building a school, or writing a book. In my case it was about handling the future as a single Mom. But for many it is about how to grab hold of something really exciting, or to chase down a dream they always wanted to pursue.

The Money Pyramid is a simple way to understand how to be lucky with money. For a pyramid to be stable balance is requited in each of the pillars. If you ignore one, then the whole thing becomes unstable.

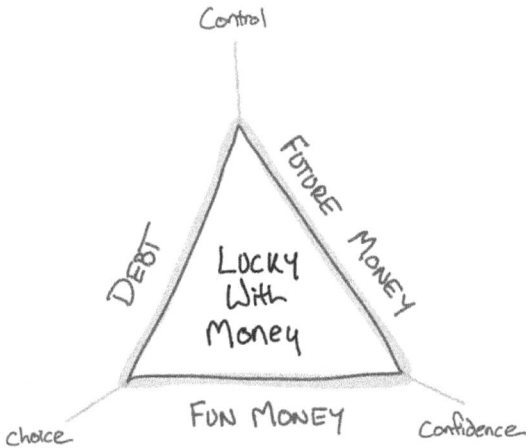

The Money Pyramid

Control

FUTURE MONEY

DEBT

LUCKY WITH Money

Choice

FUN MONEY

Confidence

It's only by mastering each of the sides of the pyramid that you'll be able to handle anything. And the result? Control, choice and confidence.

Chapter Two

DEBT

Pillar 1 – Understanding and Managing Debt

Debt is all around us. Price tags on big items now read $299 per month for this brand-new car. You don't even know what the full value of the car is, you just see the $299 per month and think that is manageable.

Debt became so normalized everyone uses it to get what they need. They don't realise how much that item actually costs them over time, and what it means in times of crisis. If you lose your job, having to pay monthly debt means you don't get anywhere. It affects your credit rating and your cashflow. Because everything ends up going towards that debt. You can't invest in your future money and you can't have fun because every cent coming in goes to someone else. You cannot enjoy the life you have to live on this earth.

Many people have a mortgage which is a better debt than most. A loan on a car, is a loan on a depreciating asset. Whereas a loan on a house is an investment, meaning eventually the value of that house will go up, or at least stay the same or similar in most cases. You can claim your investment back.

With a loan on a car, which depreciates in value very quickly, when you sell your vehicle, you will have a balance the vehicle will not cover. With credit card debt, the high interest rates mean people get themselves into holes they can't get out of.

The difference between good and bad debt is whether you are making use of it for your future good, or just for something you need to use today that will cost you significantly more. Structuring and understanding your debt is incredibly important.

The other part is how to manage money stress because we stress about the scarcity of money. We will talk about debt planning and making your way out of debt, so you can see a brighter future for yourself. Finally, once you get out of debt, we talk about how to reward yourself.

Pillar 2 – Future Money

Future money is where your emergency fund lives. It is the money saved for those unexpected items, and for your future goals.

When you have a big goal, like a trip to Australia, you have something to look forward to. You will be motivated to put money towards that trip because you look forward to it. The future money or investments help you reach your big hairy audacious goals (BHAGs).

The real question for your investments is, where do you want to go?

You can start an investment with $20. You don't have to have millions of dollars to start an investment. The key is putting money in consistently, so it grows over time. As you watch it grow, it will feel good and encourage you to put more money into your investments and pay down your debts. You will have more cash flow to keep putting towards your future money.

It is less about which stocks to buy, or whether you should invest in a particular asset class, and more about consistent habits and developing a lucky money mindset about the future.

In this pillar we will talk about how to identify those goals, create, and then execute a plan. Then we need to review and revisit what we are doing, so it is continuously aligned to our goals and what is important to us and our families.

Pillar 3 – Fun Money

Fun money is the reason we all go to work. We want to have fun and create memories with our families. If we even have a small amount of fun money per month, like $100, it keeps everything going so you can continue to have fun.

It is like having a strict diet with no cheat days; you are definitely going to cheat and fall off the wagon. But if you build some cheat days in, or in this case, fun money, you'll stay focused on your path and continue doing what you are doing.

You can have fun if you keep the cycle going, pay down the debt, and invest in the future. Then you create more memories, alleviate stress for your family, and continue on.

Not everyone can dive straight into fun money, so we will show you how to have fun that is cheap, easy, and everyone can be involved in. We will also talk about big hairy audacious goals (BHAGs) for your financial future. We will talk about how we should talk about money in a positive way. We often talk about it negatively. But by acknowledging our money wins, we attract more to ourselves.

Finally, we will talk about how memories are the best investment, and the types of memories that will live with you forever.

Our trip to Disneyland was such a great example of something that has paid dozens of times over the investment of money we made.

The Consequences of Bad Money Management

For people who don't get the debt pillar right, they experience no progress. They feel like they are on a hamster wheel going round and round. It is a disheartening place to be.

If you have made no investment in the future money pillar, it is hard to see a bright future.

We know that if we don't do things that are important or meaningful to us with our fun money, we feel like we have no life, and epic sadness can come over us. We wonder what the point of it all is. That is no way to show up for your children, partners, or friends.

Many people come to me saying they feel they are going nowhere, they can't see a bright future, and they are certainly not having a life. But when we get these pillars right, we get control over our future and feel luckier with money. This beautiful sense of confidence in what we can achieve starts to show itself.

How to Manage Money Stress

A lot of people are stressed about money because they don't know to whom or how much they owe. It is important to organize your debt, write it down so you can actually see it and get a handle on it. Sometimes we think we have a lot of debt and it is overwhelming, but when we actually see it, we might think, it's not so bad, I can crush this!

It might be a long list and it might overwhelm you, but at least you know the number and can start working towards the end goal, which is making that number zero. A lot of the stress around money is because people don't know where it is all going. Having a budget and writing down where every dollar goes. Then looking at places you can cut things, like subscriptions you may have forgotten about, or gym memberships you no longer use. This can make a big difference. Even a $10 cut in your bill will help you, as that's $10 per month more than you had before.

Many people are so stressed they don't want to know about it. They put the blinkers on which is likely a large cause of stress for most people. Having it out there and not being able to identify how much it is or having any plan to deal with it is a cause of stress.

Couples and Money Stress

Confronting what you owe, looking closely at what you spend, and understanding it all is much less stressful than not knowing. Once you have it out in front of you, you can deal with it. You can make choices and decide what your future looks like.

Most married people fight about debt and money. A major reason for marital arguments and breakdowns is money stress. Someone might be hiding debt from the other person which can cause a strain on the family. If you partner is a spend-a-holic, and you are stressed by the spending, this will be an issue. Sitting together, identifying that stress, creating a budget and working on it together can help alleviate some of that stress.

Sleepless Nights

When you are stressed about money and constantly thinking about it, it can affect your sleep as well as your state of mind. There is a commercial here for a debt consolidation place where it says:

"Is debt weighing you down? Is it on your shoulders?"

You can tell which people are stressed about money and which ones are not. It really affects your whole mental health, your insides, the health of your body and all of that. It takes a toll on you.

Really managing that stress and getting a hold on your money will help you physically as well as mentally and emotionally in your relationship.

Unhelpful Messages

The world tells us today that everything can be financed and that is totally normal. The message is: everyone is going into debt. We need to have that boat, we need that new car, we need that Louis Vuitton bag… People want things that are beyond their control and beyond their needs.

Managing money stress is two things: having a positive mindset around money that you can deal with it, and actively getting educated about your financial position. Whether it is understanding the true value of that Louis Vuitton bag you just put on your credit card, by the time you pay it off or getting a handle on the true cost of that car beyond the $299 per month. When you add it all up, it is more than you would pay for a car or bag.

We need to start being curious and questioning. What is that $10 per month for? Do I really need this? Many people think if they look closely, it will increase their stress. But they are already stressed about it by ignoring it. If we start looking at what is going on, and get curious about the solutions possible for us, it makes it more manageable.

My Rendezvous with Debt

We didn't have a lot of debt, but we had a lot of credit cards. I kept getting credit card statements with zero balances, but it really stressed me there were cards out there I didn't know about.

I pulled my credit report, reviewed each one to see which benefits I liked, and cancelled all of the ones I no longer wanted. In the world we live in, if you go to a hockey game and want a new jersey, you have to apply for a credit card to get the jersey. Then you accumulate these credit cards because you wanted something for that credit card.

It causes clutter in your wallet and mailbox you don't really need. Many of them, even with a zero balance have some kind of annual fee, or a monthly minimum you need to pay to access that line of credit, so if you are not using it, this can fall into the category of bad debt.

List out your forms of debt from the smallest amount to the largest amount and then the interest rate. For example, Visa Card $500 @ 21%. If you throw an extra $50 on it each month you will pay it off pretty quickly and feel successful. Then you will want to continue to pay the next one off.

It is always good to attack your smallest one first, because you will get rid of it really fast. That's an extra couple of hundred bucks or so you can save or start putting towards the next step. It is a good, quick win for you, and you will feel motivated to continue.

When you clear a debt, it is a dopamine hit. You feel good and want to feel like this again. They call it the snowball method because it just keeps going and going like a snowball. The snowball method is positive because you might even be getting the same level of dopamine as getting that Louis Vuitton bag or other new thing you want.

What if we replace that dopamine hit with the dopamine hit of removing some of these debts? The future payoff is enormous relative to the future payoff of those pair of jeans you will be sick of in a few months' time.

Debt Planning

If you want to pay off debt, you should use this snowball method. But if you need to go into debt, really plan out what the future might look like. If you don't need that mortgage for 25 years, then maybe choose a shorter term, 15 years if you really want to be aggressive and good with your money. Ask yourself curiously how long you want to be in debt for. If you are 25 right now, do you really want to be 50 and still paying a mortgage? Those are the things you want to consider when it comes to debt planning.

Most people don't plan. It's an impulse. It is that car I wanted, and I am so happy about the car, I forgot about the debt attached. I will be paying off for the next five or six years on an asset that will depreciate. If that asset has an accident, I won't get my funds back for what I paid on the loan.

The banker or finance company will tell you that most people finance their car for five years, or most people do a 25-year amortization mortgage, and you just do that. But you need to think about what you want for your life and what your future will look like.

It is a sure bet the bank is not recommending something that disadvantages them and is advantageous to you. So, ask whether it is right for you or not. Does this suit where you want to go? Or does this get in the way?

Also question why the finance company or car dealership is pushing me towards the brand new car, when maybe I could buy a couple of models older for a lot cheaper. Why are they pushing you to a 25-year amortization versus a 15-year amortization?

Business Debt

Sometimes you can write business debt off, but you need to consider the state of your business, and what happens if the income from your business is gone? What happens to that debt you accumulated for your business? Interest doesn't cost you anything technically because you can write it off. But if you lose the income, what will that debt cost you? How will you repay it? Does it mean you now have to extend your mortgage to pay off that business debt?

The core principle with business debt is that you are taking it on and can claim the debt expense as a business expense. It is a tax-deductible item.

We read in the newspaper that people should take on more debt in this circumstance, or this company is borrowing millions to do that, but that is not necessarily relevant to us.

Occasionally I hear of a friend whose accountant tells them they are earning too much money and need to go and buy a car. Sometimes that advice is urban legend, so when you hear of urban legends like that, it is good to look at it from a different perspective.

Mindful Spending

If you are grateful for your money, then you will be mindful and cherish it. You will want it to go somewhere you feel gratitude towards that spending.

If you approach it with a mindset of gratefulness and really think about it, that near new model is going to be okay. Is it going to do the job you need it to versus that brand new version which will cost you a lot more, but depreciate much faster?

Celebrating Small Wins

When you celebrate wins, you end up with a mindset of being lucky with money. You feel like you did something and are on a roll. You're doing good and you are motivated to keep going.

It might not be something you want to tell everyone you just paid off $5,000, but maybe you put up a picture on your wall or cut up the card and celebrate you got rid of it. It will help you feel good, lucky, that you have made a great accomplishment, and should push on and start the circle again.

Celebrating creates more abundance and prevents that scarcity mindset that your money is going to end from creeping in. It makes you feel like it is a circle; the circle of life, the circle of money that will come back to you. You will feel good about it. Your mindset will be very different when it comes to spending money.

There is an enormous amount of scientific research around the effect of gratitude on people's level of happiness. The simple act of being grateful has a biochemical reaction in our brain almost the same as taking an antidepressant. It increases the serotonin uptake in your brain to almost the same point of taking medicine.

Celebrating wins has a true effect on your level of happiness by being grateful for the progress you're making. By being grateful for the lessons you are learning in this book, you are contributing every single day to increased happiness, and increased feeling of being lucky with money.

Chapter Three

FUTURE MONEY

Future money is investment. In order to achieve future money, we need a goal plan. We need to understand what our short, mid, and long-term goals are. That way we can tell our money where to go and what to do based on these goals.

A short-term goal could be a vacation. You need to look at how much that vacation will cost, when you are planning on going on that vacation, then break it down over the time period. It could be $50 per month for the next two years to have enough for that vacation. Really break down the goals over a time period so you have them small and clean, and you can tell your money what to do for you.

It is a shift in thinking. Most people think their money tells them where to go and they are not in control of it. When you tell your money where to go, you gain that control. There is an end goal for your money. It might be your children's education you put a certain amount away for each month so you are not stressed when you get close to that time and have to scrounge, because you started saving from the day they were born. Over 18 years you saved and your money has been working for you.

Most people get scared when they hear the word 'investment.' They think of risk and all of the bad stories they have heard.

"I bought this stock, it tanked, and I lost all my money." Or "I put my money in the stock market and lost everything."

They are scared. But they are scared because they are uncertain what will happen.

There are lots of things people look at as investments other than stocks or putting their money in the bank. Many people start businesses as investments. If that doesn't go well, people lose their money, and it can be a difficult thing. A better definition of investment is actually you telling your money where to go in an organised way so you are clear on what you are working towards.

Myth 1 – You Have to Have a Lot of Money Before you Start Investing

You don't need to have a lot of money to start investing. My client and her husband just started investing and they like real estate. Her husband has health issues so he can't get life insurance and says real estate is his life insurance for his wife if anything happens to him. She can relinquish a property and have money to live on.

He did that, but she always wanted to do some investing and learn about the stock market, but she was scared. I asked her what she was willing to risk, and she started with $50. We opened a self-directed portfolio through one of the major banks and started dabbling.

She started having a bit more fun with it and feeling good. It is like going to a casino: you start with $50 at the slot machine because you are really scared, but then you get on a roll. Then you feel you can do a little more. She started to do really well. When she had wins and her money started to grow, she wanted to take it all out and be done with it. Like at the casino, she had fun, she did it, and then she's leaving the casino.

I convinced her to reinvest it now she had more money to play with, continue to grow it, and now she is established. The fear got lost after she started doing it. As you can see, just need $50 to get started, and if you are going to do something like Bitcoin, that is all you need to get started there as well.

There are lots of options for people to start having their money work for them instead of working for money. This is what investment is about, and it is a critical mind shift to make.

If you give money with gratefulness, you are grateful to your money. If you gratefully give to this investment, you would hope you get abundance with that, it comes back, and it grows. But if you give it with a scarcity or scared mindset, you might not do so well.

It is like when you jump into a pool and tell yourself it will be warm, then it won't be that scary. If you think about how cold it will be when you jump, it is going to be cold.

The way you think about investment is important, and it is okay to start small, learn along the way, and develop your skills. Investing money and making it work for you is quite simply a new skill that is not taught in many places.

It is important to stay invested. That is all part of it. It is a long-term plan. There will be daily dips, but your vision is for 10 years from now, so don't worry about those daily dips. If you keep contributing to it on an ongoing basis, it will have a compounding effect which will create your snowball and really start growing.

For most people the fear comes because they might lose some of their hard-earned money. But as soon as there are a few wins, they want to take it out of the stock market for example. But a better way to look at it is as a long-term investment, and the vast amount of investments over a long-term period return positively.

Myth 2 – I Don't Have Enough Spare Money to Start Investing

For people who don't feel like they can spare enough to start investing, I say maybe sell a couple of things in your house, pick up some extra shifts somewhere, drive Uber for a bit and see if you can earn some extra cash to earmark for investing.

When you get that extra paycheck, it shouldn't go towards your bills, it goes to the investments you want to do, so you start getting into the system, start investing and getting your money to grow and work for you.

Most people can look around their home, find things they no longer use and sell them on eBay to get $1,000 together. I do a purge of my house and even purge my clothing. My daughter and I do a clothing purge every season, and one season we made $700. There are lots of things in our homes we may not use anymore, but someone else will.

You can use places like Facebook Marketplace, Kijiji and so on. It is definitely worth trying to drum up a bit of money selling some of your old junk.

If you are thinking 100% of your wages are already accounted for so you can't start investing, look at that old sports equipment, musical gear, furniture, clothes, or whatever. You could do a yard sale. This money becomes the beginning of your investment, because if you earn $1,000 selling your clothing and purging, that is a way anyone can become an investor.

Myth 3 – Investing is Risky

People don't know what they are doing, so they fear the unknown. The stock market does come with risks, and if you want higher than average returns, you have to take a bit of extra risk. But if you take no risk, the return will be low. If you want to do better than inflation, you have to take a little bit of risk.

When people hear the word 'risk' they think they are going to lose everything. There is a chance, but it is not going to be like your savings account which gets 2% every month. It is the risk of not knowing what you are going to get. But you also don't know how much you are going to make over time. You need to see it as a long-term investment. You shouldn't worry about or even look at the day-to-day fluctuations. Look at it monthly just to make sure everything is going in the right direction. If you look at it every day you will have heart palpitations which won't be good for you.

There are many different classes of investment. Many people look at investment like these wild, crazy Hollywood movies of people making and losing millions overnight. The reality is every person who invests in anything can do so at a risk level that aligns to them.

For example, you can put money into the bank and get a very low return, but it is a guaranteed return. You can put your money in stocks and get a slightly higher return. You can put it in new technologies and venture capital funds and potentially get a really great return, but it comes with greater risk.

Identify your appetite for risk and look at those kinds of investments. Houses are the primary asset most people think of. In most countries your home is a tax-free investment which is significant. If you buy your home, do it up, sell it, and get a bigger one, or renovate it, you are paying down your loan while your house goes up in value. When you sell your house, the government will not tax you on any gains. That is significant because as a commercial investor you have to pay some sort of tax for whatever gains you make on your investment.

Home ownership is important, but I wouldn't suggest moving into a house to be poor. Make sure you buy a house that's within your means. Don't buy that million-dollar property your friends are buying if you can't afford it right now. It is a risk because it is a big investment. But it is a long-term investment which will appreciate in value. As you pay down the loan, the value will go up and you can capitalize on some of that equity when you're ready to sell the property.

Investment is about future money, whether it is building equity into your home by paying down the loan, investing in other companies via the stock market, or even investing in your own business. The question is how do you make your money work harder than you work? That is what investment is all about.

Investment is all about making your money work harder than you do.

Goals and Money

Sometimes we don't tie money and goals together. If you want to retire at 50, what do you have to do to get to that point? A lot of people don't know. You have to work backwards. What will your cost of living look like when you are retired at 50? How much do you need on a monthly basis just to survive, pay your mortgage, rent, food, and so on? What kind of fun stuff do you want to do?

Then think if you are 50 years old and going to live until 80 years old, what is that monthly cost over 30 years? That is how much you need to have saved up. So, if you really want to retire at 50 and have a certain lifestyle, can you achieve that? Or do you need to go back and tweak your goals a bit?

The Goals Timeline Exercise

This goal timeline exercise breaks down goals into short, medium, and long-term goals. A lot of people only focus on retirement and maybe don't do anything else with their money. They just save and save, but they don't live their life.

They have no short-term goals. You need to have short-term goals, like a year from now you would like to go on this vacation, buy a new vehicle, or pay off this debt.

A mid-term goal could be within the next three to five years. Perhaps it's a big vacation you want to take to Australia or something really big you want to do. If you have money around goals and timeframes, you will be more successful reaching those goals.

Long-term goals are usually retirement, kids' education, and big-ticket items like a retirement home in Dubai.

Most people only think about what is right in front of them when it comes to goals. Use this worksheet to consider what you'd like to achieve in different time horizons.

The GOALS TIMELINE

SHORT 12 mths	MEDIUM 3 yrs	LONG 10 yrs

Setting goals is about identifying what we want, because most people just go through day by day, turning up to work, paying the bills, and running the kids around, without actually thinking about what we actually want to achieve.

How do you see your life? What do you want to do with your children? What are the things on your bucket list? How do these all fit into your short, mid, and long-term goals?

Goals and Vision Boards

Vision boards are amazing too. I set one up on my computer today. They help you stay focused. What is in front of you every day is where you are going. What is to your right is money, to your left is goals, and what is behind you is your past. Set one up somewhere you can see it, whether it is a picture of you retired sipping coconuts on the beach, then determine how you want to get those goals.

If you are struggling, open some magazines or flip through Pinterest, see what strikes you as something you want to do, and really start flowing that imagination again. If you always wanted a car, go find a picture of the car you want or the holiday you would like.

Most people put their vision boards right by their bed so they see it when they wake up in the morning, or in their office so they can see it throughout the day. The brain takes it in and you don't have to stand in front of it. You can just walk by it, your brain will pick it up, and start creating it in your life. It will happen with you just walking by and seeing those images every day.

For example, if you are trying to lose weight and achieve washboard abs, have a picture of yourself looking like that. What will happen is, subconsciously, you will ask yourself if you really need that extra muffin or whether you could just have a cup of tea instead.

The Bucket list exercise is a great way to expand your thinking. We've made some suggestions in the worksheet, but please start making your own and filling it with what inspires you.

The BUCKET-LIST

The LIST	Details
Where I would Live	
How I spend my time	
Vacations - Adventures	
Purchases & Toys	
Hobbies - skills	
Big Dreams	
Charity - Impact	
family	
Education	
Something that thrills me	
Investments	

You will not get the washboard abs without doing the exercises, but it will tweak something in your brain. I was overweight after I had my daughter and was in a diet program. They told me every time I went to the fridge or pantry to just say, "stop." It jerks your brain to assess why you are there instead of mindlessly going to the fridge. It stops your brain from doing what you used to do mindlessly.

We know what we focus on becomes a radar. For example, if you bought a yellow sports car and drove it out of the showroom. Then everywhere you go for the next week, you would see the same make, model, and colour as yours. You would notice there were suddenly a lot of them on the road. In reality they were there all along, but your radar wasn't up for it.

We see that when we get the latest phone. We start noticing other people have the same colour, styling, and brand. That is your brain's natural radar looking for similarities. The reason the vision board works is we are pre-loading that radar and trying to get our brain focused on the kind of things that actually are aligned to what we want to do.

Chapter Four

PLANNING TO BE LUCKY WITH MONEY

You need to have a roadmap or plan to get you where you want to go. If you want to retire at 50, what does that look like? If you are not working, where are your savings going to come from? What is your lifestyle? What is the minimum amount you can live on? What is the life expectancy in your country for your gender and ethnicity?

You can be 21 and have a blueprint to retire at 50. Between 21 and 50, you know you have to save this much every month to reach that target.

A goal without a timeline is just a wish. Planning is about making your goals concrete. Planning is about stopping it from being a wish and turning it into a reality. In order to that, it needs a map and steps along the way to create that.

Don't Want / Do Want Exercise

It is always easier to write down what you don't want. Everyone knows what lifestyle they don't want to have, so start with your "Don't want" list first.

You don't want to be broke, you don't want to be over your head in debt, and so on. Then you need a blueprint in order to not be broke, or over your head in debt.

Dump everything out of your brain you "Don't Want" on the right-hand side and get really specific. It might be you don't want to live in a location, or do this type of work, or be single, or married. Brain dump everything you don't want. Our brains are hardwired to identify risk and what we don't want. Most people find it easy to fill up several pages of what they don't want.

It is harder working backwards from that list. On the left we are saying, in order to not have that what do I want? We really work our brain hard by doing this exercise. We tap into this natural cycle starting with the "Don't Wants."

Now start building the "Do Want" list. At the end of this exercise, you will see some really clear things you want. Then your job is to prioritize those and start fitting them into a timeframe. Is this a short-term, 12-month goal, a mid-term three-to-five-year goal, or a long-term 10 year goal. Where does it fit in? What do I need to do to make this happen?

Most people don't have a plan, and all of a sudden, they are in their 40s, thinking about retirement, and have to do this catch-up process. It can be done, but it is a lot of hard work, if you have lived your life not thinking about the future.

Don't Want - Do Want

Don't Want	Do Want

There is no such thing as a perfect plan. There is no way to do it wrong, except to not do one at all. By far 99% of people don't have a plan whatsoever. It can be a sticky note on the fridge, a fancy spreadsheet, it doesn't matter, just start making a plan.

The Pitfalls of Planning

One of the biggest pitfalls when you are investing in the markets is taking out long-term investments when there are dips in the market a few years too early. The economy has ups and downs over a few years. People take out their money, because they think they have already lost too much, and they are scared. They want to save what they do have left, versus remembering that their plan for that money was not for right now, but for five years from now.

If you take it out, you cannot recuperate that money again. You actually want to buy when things are down and put more money in because everything is on clearance. Smart investors put more money in when the market is in the downturn so they can capitalize on the clearance prices.

Executing the plan can be different as we are fighting our psychological aversion to risk.

Staying committed to the plan is an area many people go wrong with. Life happens. So, if there is a health reason you need to deviate from the plan, once everything is back to normal, you need to autocorrect, and hopefully make up for lost time.

If you were used to putting in $50 a month but had to stay out for a couple of years, try now going up to $100 to make up for that lost time. Stay committed to it and stay on track, because life happens, and new shiny things happen. It is attractive to take that $50 back for instant gratification right now instead of 10 years from now using that $50.

Consistency is the key. It is not important you are the world's smartest investor, or that you have the most money, it is important to remain consistent in executing the plan. The reason that is so powerful in investing is that we talk about compound interest.

If you put $1,000 in and get 10% interest, now you have $1,100. Ten percent interest on $1,100 is more than what the original was, so over a period of time, one of the most powerful forces in building any kind of wealth is compound interest. It works against you in debt, but for you in investment. When it stops working for you is when you stop being consistent in working towards and executing the plan.

Review and Revisit

People often think they should cash out in a downturn, but it might just be a course correction that you have to do. Maybe you thought your risk tolerance was higher than it actually is. Rather than pulling everything out, talk to your advisor, revisit your goals, and rejig it. It will work itself out again.

Consistency is key. Remain consistent in executing your investment plan.

Also revisit your goals again because things may have changed. Maybe your goal was to climb Mount Everest, but now you are not healthy enough to do it. You might change that to something else. You might need some medication, or to change your house to be more equipped for you. You want to always revisit the goals and plan to make sure your risk tolerance matches your investments as well.

It is not a set and forget approach. You can't make one decision one day, then completely ignore it forever. Smart investors constantly review and assess how each of them is going. But they don't make knee jerk, fear-based reactions. They realign everything to whatever is happening in their life at that time.

When September 11, 2001 (9/11) happened, the markets crashed. People who were retiring at that time saw their money tank and it was tough. Many took their money out in that September or October low, but if they had waited a couple of months, the market not only picked up, it doubled what it was. If they had stayed invested, they would have made more money versus taking the loss. You don't hear from the people in 2002 who stayed invested and doubled their money.

Diversify

It is important to make sure you are diversified and all your eggs are not in the same basket. If your eggs were all in airline stock, maybe it wasn't a good thing. If you had airline stock, bank stocks, energy stocks, and were nicely diversified, that airline stock would have tanked, but the bank stocks might have picked up and course corrected for you.

It's like your Mom tells you, you want to have your eggs in different baskets in case one of the baskets breaks. Then you still have other ones to lean on. If you are only invested in the housing market and the market tanks, or airline stocks and the airline stocks tank, you are in trouble.

But if you are diversified, you can stay the course of the housing crisis. Stay invested in the housing market because you are diversified elsewhere, and it is not such a big dip in your portfolio to your net worth.

A regular investing experience is basically a dollar cost advantage. If you are putting money in on a regular basis, you will buy the stock at highs and lows. It will average out and your book value will be lower than your current value of the stock. What you bought it at is always going to be lower than what the current value is of the stock. That's normal.

If you go through a bank or an advisor, they have guidelines they have to follow, and can't put you in those high-risk things. For example, if you say you only want to buy gold, they have to get approval from the Securities Commission to let you purchase only gold because there are checks and balances through the system. If you follow a typical banking guideline, and when they ask you questions you answer truthfully, you should be able to reach your goals for your investment. Just ensure you don't panic pay when the dips come along.

Many people say when your taxi driver gives you stock market tips, it is time to get out of the stock market. You shouldn't get your investment decisions from the public; you should look at your own risk profile. What is your appetite for risk? What are your goals? How do you align what you are doing with that? And then speak to a professional.

Investing as a Solo Mom

I learned I am someone who needs my investing done for me automatically. I'm not a natural saver or someone who thinks about savings. If I don't think about it, it doesn't happen.

When my pay cheque comes in, a certain amount every month automatically goes into my investment I don't know about. That way I have peace of mind it's done. It goes in and the money starts working for me.

I also visit my planner each year and we review my goals. It is great because he asks me things like whether I am dating, if we need to make changes for health, or things like that. They are trained to ask you these questions to make sure your plan is still working for you.

Investing Tips for Single Women

There are three things I suggest for single women getting into investment:

1. Automate, automate, automate! It is one less thing you have to do. You have to take care of your kids, make school lunches, and so on.

2. Visit your financial planner once a year. Make sure your money can continue to do what you want it to do for you. If you decide to take a sabbatical from work, your money has to work for you, and start

    paying you. You advisor needs to know to do that for you.

3. Make sure your risk tolerance is the risk tolerance that works for you. My risk tolerance was mostly joint investments. My risk tolerance was higher when I was married, but when I went back and revisited it, it became lower. Make sure your appetite for risk is being met.

Your goals change. Perhaps as a married couple your goals were to retire together in Dubai. Now you are single, your goal might be to retire tomorrow and travel the rest of the world. Make sure your goals are yours now and not your old joint goals.

Chapter Five

FUN MONEY

Diets often fail because people don't incorporate cheat days. If you incorporate cheat days, you know if you are good all week, every Saturday you can have your Oreos. The same thing goes for fun money. If you are staying on budget, calculate some fun time into your budget, and reward yourself for being good and tight on your budget.

If you're paying down your debt and putting some money into investments, always make sure you have a little fun money. If you are not incorporating fun into your day-to-day life, you will fall off track and go into debt to go on some major vacation you don't need.

Cheap, Easy Fun

Cheap, easy fun makes sure you enjoy yourself every day, but doesn't have to hurt your bank account. Play board games, dig out the puzzles and do those as a family, and play quizzing games with your kids. My daughter used to love playing *Would you rather…?* And we played it all the time.

Do something outside. Go for a walk in the park, or for a hike. It doesn't cost anything but is still fun. Look at ways to be creative with things. Go window shopping, walk around downtown, and explore your local town. If you live in a warm climate, it costs nothing to go to the beach. In cold climates, it costs nothing to build a snowman.

After my husband passed away, I didn't want me or my daughter to live in a doom and gloom world. I wanted to make sure we had fun and she had as normal life as she could. Her friends were doing similar things. Kids don't care what you do, just that you do something together. If we went tobogganing, that is cheap and easy, and she would tell her friends about it. Spending time with them versus buying things is always more important to them. They will appreciate that no matter what.

We try to have fun every day. After I finish this section, we are going to watch *The Bachelor*. That is our fun, bonding time together. We have a dog now, so we play little games with him, like *Keep Away* and he loves that. We need a little bit of fun so she feels like she had a good day. You don't need expensive things to have fun.

Big, Hairy, Audacious Goals (BHAGs)

I ask my clients if money was no object, what would they do with their life? A lot of people say they would travel the world or have a million-dollar house with a pool and sports car outside. But often it relates to creating memories with their families.

If money was no object, it would be giving back to people and charities, working from home, or even not working and having quality time with their children.

Thinking about money being no object helps you imagine what your goals could be once your money starts working for you. When I ask people about their goals without this question of limitless money, people usually limit their goals because they consider how much it will cost and start over thinking it.

If you eliminate the cost factor, you find out your true goals; what you really want to do. You figure out who you are as a person and your true desires and dreams.

When we start dreaming big, all of a sudden when we really think about it, it doesn't sound so scary anymore. Travelling the world might become seeing the seven wonders of the world, then break it down more. It opens our minds to what we can do, and then we can get our money to work for us to make it happen.

It is a vision board multiplied by a factor of 100. When we stop to get really excited about what we can potentially do then reverse engineer our goals.

What would your house look like if money was no object? Would you have a pool? A butler? How many bedrooms would there be? What would each bedroom have in it? Would each bedroom have a bathroom? We dig deep into what it would look like. What kind of car would you have? How many? What school would your kids go to?

It is about taking the limits off. Even if you had $100 million, as you get further down on this worksheet, you might start limiting what you write because you are thinking about things with a dollar value. There should be no limits. If they come to your mind, eliminate them.

What did you dream about when you were a kid? Was your dream job playing with purple unicorns all day? Maybe no one told you there were no purple unicorns and you dreamed about them all the time.

There are prompts on this list about your house, car, lifestyle, charity time, legacy and so on, but there are a few blank spaces for you to really explore any aspect you would like to without any limits.

Once we develop the list, we can start taking our first steps towards those goals. Rather than believing our goals are unachievable, we can actually start making progress towards them.

B.H.A.G list (Big, hairy, Audacious, Goal)

If Money Was Not a Constraint, What would You do?

Hoose	
lifestyle	
Vechiles	
School	
Toys	
Adventues	
Dreams	
Legacy	
Travel	
Charity	

Celebrate Wins!

One of the biggest progresses I made was buying my first house. I never owned a property before, so it was a big win for me. We celebrated by having a nice housewarming party where people could come and celebrate with us. It was a fun day where people looked at the house and brought gifts.

Celebrating is not about the gifts, but about sharing your wins with people. They don't have to be big milestones. It could be you paid off a $50 credit card. You should celebrate that because it is a big feat that others may not be doing. Others are drowning in debt and you are paying of a credit card. That is huge.
Celebrating wins is huge to keep you motivated and moving towards your goals.

People commonly focus on all of their problems and rarely look at their progress and wins. We look at how much we still have to pay from that credit card or loan, but not what they have already achieved. They miss the opportunity for that dopamine hit that comes even from doing the little things.

I always make my bed every morning because that is one win I have a day. Now maybe I can do my 30-minute workout because I already had my one win for the day. It keeps you awake, motivated, and gives you that kickstart to do something else. You crave more wins.

I've never been a glass half empty person. I have always been very optimistic. That may have resulted in me being *Lucky with Money*. It was just my view on life. My Mom always said not to cry over spilt milk. If something bad happened, we would just see what else could be done.

I don't like negative talk. If someone has a problem, I always want to know what they are going to do about it. You can dwell and have self-pity for the problem, or you can start taking action to resolve the problem. There are things you can't change like a diagnosis about your husband. I could have wallowed in grief and been sad, but instead I switched into, "What are we going to do about it?" mode. We couldn't change it, so what were we going to do about it so it wasn't such a bad experience.

Highest Returning Investment

Money people will tell you the highest return on investments are from equities. In fact, creating important memories with people that are close to you is the highest return on investment for all the money you spend.

Taking your child to Disneyland will cost a fair bit of money. That will be difficult in the short-term because of the money you have to put in, but you will all remember that for the rest of your lives. You will talk about it every month remembering when you saw Goofy, or when you went on this ride or to that show. You will share it forever. That is a return on investment.

Your investment advisor can't measure it, so it is hard to talk to them about it, but these memories pay off forever.

When my husband was diagnosed with cancer and told he had six months to live, we had to decide whether to go to Phoenix, pay a bunch of money for medical treatment that may or may not work, or take our daughter to Disneyland. She was five and we always wanted to take her there.

Many of our friends and family thought we were making the wrong decision to forgo medical treatment. They thought we should have taken the chance to save his life. But my husband was adamant he wanted to be the one to take her to Disneyland, so we went. If you talk to my daughter about her Dad, she will always tell you a Disneyland story. It has appreciated in value from when we actually went until now. Every year that goes by, we talk about that trip. We went on so many other trips before that, but it is her fondest memory.

Using money to spend time with the people you love could also be about coaching your child in a sport, watching your local sporting team together, or some other activity you all enjoy. Investing time and money in that experience will appreciate in value at an exponential rate over their lifetime.

Nostalgia Bias

I recently learned a concept called the Nostalgia Bias. Think about the biggest purchase you ever made, like a car. The highest value you get from that car is on the day you purchased it. On that day your emotions are high with the new car smell and your friends appreciating it. But over time it depreciates in monetary value as well as heart value.

With your memories, the opposite is true. They appreciate in value over time. You value them more.

Getting Out of Debt

When working with me, I firstly encourage people to look at paying off their debt. You want to start actioning your debt and getting rid of it because as long as the debt is still there, you can do some of the other stuff, but it will just keep piling up. You can do this while building your investments and still having fun, but eliminate as much debt as possible.

I offer one on one coaching and group coaching sessions for people. I do a free 30-minute consultation which can be booked through my website to see if we are a fit for the programs I offer.

I love working with widowed Moms, looking to find joy and start really living their life purpose

every day. I help them reduce stress and manage
their money so they can start their lives again.

Chapter Six

THE REAL MOM'S MONEY MATRIX

This tool will help you to see clearly where you are right now and what your next move needs to be. And I'll show you how to get more help.

The vertical axis on the money matrix measures consumption. Do you spend without thinking? At the top of it we have conscious consumption, and at the bottom we have unconscious consumption. Are you thinking about what you are buying, or just doing things to keep up with the Joneses? The horizontal axis is about whether you are spending within or outside of your budget. Most people find themselves in one of these zones at one point.

Which Zone are you in?

If you are unconsciously consuming and getting things to keep up with the Joneses using credit, we call that the *Disaster Zone*. You are outside of your budget and not getting joy out of the purchases you really want.

If we are still in a bit of unconscious spending, but we are spending within our budget, that is the *Reflex Zone*. Most widowed Moms are in this zone. We often find ourselves overcompensating for lack of time with the children by eating out because it is difficult to cook meals. You might be within your budget, but it won't be sustainable. Eventually you will move to the other side above budget in the *Disaster Zone.*

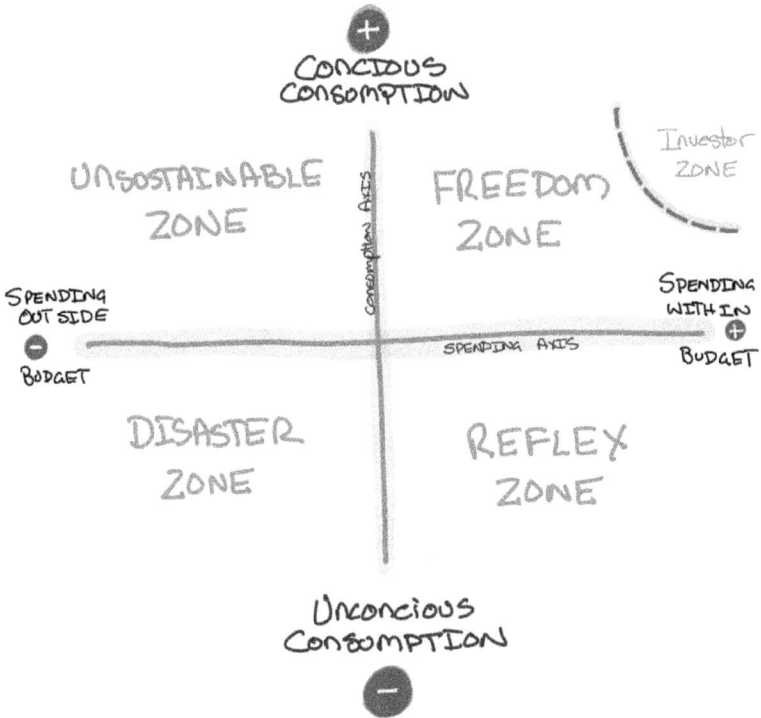

The Real Mom's
MONEY MATRIX

CONCIOUS CONSUMPTION (+)

UNSOSTAINABLE ZONE

FREEDOM ZONE

Investor ZONE

Consumption Axis

SPENDING OUT SIDE BUDGET (−)

SPENDING AXIS

SPENDING WITH IN BUDGET (+)

DISASTER ZONE

REFLEX ZONE

Unconcious Consumption (−)

That leads people to the *Unsustainable Zone* where they become more conscious of what they are doing but have tipped outside of their means. Perhaps the insurance has run out, or they are not working for six months, but they are still conscious of the spending even if it is outside the budget.

Where we want to be is conscious about what is important to us so we spend money on the right things and stick to our budget. That is the great intersection of conscious consumption and spending within your means, the *Freedom Zone.* As you begin to work deeper and deeper into that zone, you move over to the *Investor Zone* which helps your money work harder than you do.

I work with Moms, particularly widowed ones to identify where they are at in the Real Mom's Money Matrix, then help them put in place what they need to move. The next step might just be moving from the *Disaster Zone* to one of the other zones, then gradually moving into the *Freedom Zone.*

WORKSHEET: Which Zone are you In Right Now?

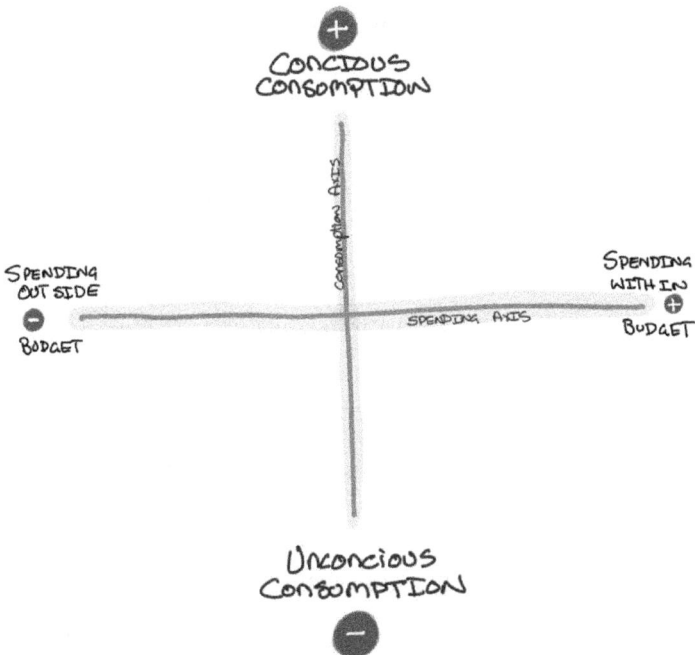

CONCIOUS CONSUMPTION

Consumption AXIS

SPENDING OUT SIDE BUDGET

SPENDING AXIS

SPENDING WITH IN BUDGET

UNCONCIOUS CONSUMPTION

Use the worksheet above to determine where you are right now. Map yourself against the X and Y axis.

So many widows, especially widowed moms, moms find themselves in the bottom right-hand quadrant. They may be spending within budget, but they are on autopilot, spending without really thinking about how the purchases will be valued. This is totally understandable as you are often in shock and doing the best you can, but the way to become luckier with money is to work toward the freedom zone.

The Disaster Zone

The first thing you must do is be honest about the situation you're in. Ask yourself the hard questions: is the debt keeping you up at night? are you stressed about tomorrow and putting food on the table? What you're doing is identifying the impact the disaster zone has on you, both physically and mentally.

The first step is to create a budget: identify what is coming in and what is going out. In other words, what is your actual situation at the end of the month? Do you have money left over you're just throwing away on unnecessary things? Is there nothing leftover? In each of these situations, you need to identify what you're going to do to stop spending the extra money or what you can do to create more money.

When you're in the disaster zone, the best thing you can do is my program that teaches you how to save or make $1,000 in 30 days. I'm going to tell you to start something or tell you to amplify something you're already doing.

The Reflex Zone

You're spending within your budget but you're not really thinking about where or how you're spending. There are some strategies to move out of this "unconscious spending" pattern.

Get real and honest with yourself.

Are you experiencing certain emotions that are making you spend unconsciously? Do you spend when you're sad or happy or angry or mad? What you're after is that instant gratification feeling, but then the initial emotion comes back and you're back in the vicious cycle.

What we are identifying in the reflex zone is: what is driving my spending behaviour? Are we trying to fill a gap by spending? Are we doing things without thinking about them? Once we've answered these questions, it's time to be honest and determine if this way of spending is working. If it isn't satisfying you, you're probably consuming in a completely unconscious way.

At this point, you need to find a system that works for you. Maybe it's the cash envelope system where you put a certain amount of cash in each envelope and when it's gone, it's gone. In this system, you're consciously deciding what to spend your money on and how much to dedicate to it. You can take whatever is left over and start investing it. We like the 45-45-10 rule: 45% goes toward investing, 45% goes toward debt, and 10% goes for fun. This way you can still save up for a new purse or pair of shoes or fancy dinner out and not feel guilty about spending that money. It's all about balance. The problem is we're spending without even thinking about it. By starting to think about where our money goes, we are re-aligning our spending to what's important to us.

The Unsustainable Zone

In this zone, we've chosen what to spend on, but, in reality, are living outside of our means. This zone aligns with the saying, "Keeping up with the Joneses." When you're in this zone, you need to stop and recognize that you're trying to win a race with someone or something and it's not going to help you in the long run.

It's very important to remember that someone else's financial journey is very different than yours, and that's ok. If we can learn to express gratitude rather than feel jealous when someone tells you about their new car or boat, then you'll start to see the changes in your mind. It switches your thinking from a scarcity mindset to an abundance mindset.

When you stop thinking that the cars and luxuries are limited to certain people but, rather, that there's enough money and abundance around the world for everybody, you'll start seeing changes in your life. You'll start seeing things flow in your life.

So how do we stop this race with the Joneses? Stick to your budget. Identify what's important to you. If your friend gets a new car, but you're saving for vacation, then you can still feel happy for your friend, knowing you're saving for your dream vacation. It's important to have your own "big picture" goals. Without them, you're much more easily susceptible to the "shiny object syndrome." If you keep your sights on what you're saving for, it makes it easier to say no to the things that get in your way.

The Freedom Zone

This is where you're consciously consuming, sticking to your budget, and not giving in to the shiny object syndrome. There are some important things to remember when you're in this zone.

The first is to give yourself a pat on the back for getting here. Make sure you have the systems in place to keep you successful and in this zone. Anytime money comes in, pay your living expenses, pay your bills, and whatever is left over gets applied to the *45-45-10 Rule*. Your investments can be set up so they're paying you money as well. This is the ideal circle where you're putting money in but it's also paying you out.

It's important to remember that investing can be risky, but it can also create a lot of wealth for yourself as well. Going in with your eyes open and being honest about what level of risk you're willing to take and how long you're willing to invest is part of embracing this zone.

It's much more of a sophisticated zone where you can get creative in making your money work better for you. It still requires a level of strategy and knowledge. It also requires an understanding that it is very easy to slip back into any one of the previous zones. You must be diligent and consistent, and you'll have the ability to be *Lucky with Money*.

How to get help

If you have enjoyed what you have read, and would like to have me speak at an event or hold a workshop for you,

please email me at hello@zahrakhakoo.com to set up a time for us to get together and discuss possible plans.

You can also visit my website.
www.zahrakhakoo.com
for more information, and as always you can follow me on Facebook through
facebook/zahrakhakoo or
Instagram @zahrakhakoo

I truly look forward to hearing from you and I appreciate your interest in my book.

If you would like a downloadable version of any of my worksheets or frameworks go to this link.

zahrakhakoo.com/landing/oola-finance-free-offer